Run Wild

~

N. D. Ableson

~DEDICATION~

For Rena, Leah, and Grace

~

CONTENTS

~ACKNOWLEDGEMENTS~

Thank you to my family!

Thanks to Julia H. for being my best friend and editor!

And a huge thank you to Erin Osiowy for this amazing book cover! (@YamnuskaStudios on Instagram)

~NAME PRONUNCIATIONS~

*Tiki – Tea-key

*Czar – Zar

*Stargazer – Star-gazer

*Comanche – Cuh-mon-chee

*Lula – Loo-lah

*Keiki – Keh-key

*Marco – Mar-co

*Zane – Zayn

*Mercury – Mer-cure-ee

*Lara – Lair-uh

*Marta – Mar-tuh

*Redantre – Reh-don-tray

*Tretaregon – Treh-tear-uh-gone

*Kentril – Ken-trill

~Chapter 1~
"Survive"

Czar looked up from the patch of grass he was munching and spotted a black and white mare ambling slowly down a hill. A blue roan filly trotted by her side. Czar tore after them at a canter. Tiki saw him coming and neighed in greeting.

"Hello, Czar! How are you?" Tiki asked, bobbing her black mane in the wind.

"Very well, Tiki. Hello, Stargazer. You look quite pretty today," said Czar.

Stargazer lowered her delicate face, nearly glowing from the compliment. Though she was usually a rambunctious little yearling, she had many wild flowers tucked in her mane and tail. Smiling, Stargazer whinnied her thanks to Czar.

"Thank you, Czar."

"Now then, how about a refreshing gallop down to the stream?" questioned Czar, pawing the ground in anticipation.

"Oh, Czar," teased Tiki. "I'm afraid I will never cure you of your wild nature."

"Remember, Tiki, we are all wild Mustangs! Not one bit of our blood is domestic or tame. We can run if we please!"

Without warning, Tiki took off at full gallop. Stargazer followed, stretching her long, gangly legs as far as they would go. Czar snorted and raced after them, his dark liver chestnut coat shining. They flew past a small family of horses and slowed to bid them good evening.

"Hello, Comanche!" shouted Stargazer, trotting closer to the group.

Comanche, a steel-gray stallion, lifted his head and whinnied back politely. His mate, Lula, nodded to them. Their foals, Keiki, Marko, and Zane, cantered towards Tiki and Stargazer.

"May we run with you? Arana is away with her mother Sertina and won't be back until evening," pouted fleabitten gray filly Keiki.

Arana was Keiki's best friend and was also the daughter of Tretaregon, the herd's leader. Old Tretaregon had led the herd since he was only six years old, and his stern wisdom kept the herd thriving. Keiki and Arana loved each other like sisters and were always found side by side. Marko and Zane found most of their companionship in each other, as they were twin foals.

"Of course you may, Keiki!" said Czar.

"Off to the creek, then!" shouted Tiki, already

cantering to the edge of the woods.

The rest chased after her and fought to regain the lost ground. Zane, a swift white two-year-old, drew even with the paint mare and slowly took the lead. Laughing and shouting, the horses charged into the creek and halted in the middle. Tiki rolled in the cold water until her coat was soaked. Stargazer lipped the surface of the crystal clear water and giggled at the minnows swimming between her small hooves. Zane and Marko splashed Keiki, ignoring her annoyed shrieks and pleadings. Czar drank heavily of the water before plunging all the way under. He came up spluttering and laughed heartily.

"Who wants to explore the woods? There's a small cliff up ahead with a glorious view of the sunset!" he announced, dashing onto the other side of the creek.

"I don't know, Czar. We need to be back in the

meadow before dusk and it is nearing that time of day. Stargazer needs her rest," reminded Tiki, nudging the wet filly with her velvety pink nose.

Tiki and Stargazer had been inseparable since the deadly cougar attack, only six months before, that had claimed the lives of Tiki's mother and both of Stargazer's parents. Ever since the sunset of that horror-filled day, Tiki had become like a mother to the young filly. Kentril was Tiki's father and was close in council with Tretaregon. He completely supported Stargazer and had immediately accepted her into his family.

"Come on, Tiki!" begged Czar. "We'll make it back in time!"

"Well…." started Tiki.

"Please?" four foal voices chimed in pleadingly.

Tiki sighed. "All right, but we must be back in fifteen minutes or we will be in serious trouble with Tretaregon, Kentril, and Comanche."

"Yes!" exclaimed the three stallions. Stargazer and Keiki danced excitedly in the creek, stirring up sand and shells.

"This way!" guided Czar, trotting confidently up the creek bank.

Tiki followed first and Stargazer was soon by her side. Keiki pranced alongside Czar, nodding attentively as he described the place he was taking them. Zane whispered to Marko and the two burst into boisterous laughter.

"What?" demanded Keiki, always wanting to know her brothers' inside jokes.

"Nothing!" answered Marko, faking nonchalance.

"It is something, but we're just not going to tell you," said Zane.

"Please, please, please?" begged Keiki.

The young stallions traded glances and nickered to each other, questioning.

"I don't know if you really want to hear this," Marko sighed in a taunting, sing-song tone.

"Marko!" whined Keiki. "C'mon! Just tell me! I'll give you…both my wild strawberries that I found yesterday."

"Hmmmm…." hummed Zane, pretending to

think about the proposition.

"All right! Fine!" agreed Marko.

"Finally! So…..?" prompted Keiki.

"Well, Zane whispered to me something I thought was hilarious."

Keiki snorted. "I got that much."

"He said "Marko, wouldn't it be funny if we put spiders in Redantre's bed?" Remember, now, Redantre can't stand spiders. He would wake up and find millions of creepy little eyes staring at him," finished Marko, laughing so hard that tears spilled out the corners of his eyes.

"Whaa-but-but-but that's not fair! That wasn't

funny! Now I have to give you my strawberries!"

"Exactly," chortled Marko.

Czar and Zane laughed along with him. Tiki
and Stargazer just rolled their eyes and trotted
ahead. Keiki followed them, pouting all the way
about her unfairly bought wild strawberries. The
stallions finished their joking so they could catch
up. After climbing for a few minutes, Czar stopped
suddenly at a place where the trees opened up to
a large flat rock.

"Whoa. I can see everything from here!"
gaped Stargazer, soft brown eyes wide.

Czar stepped forward cautiously.

"Be careful near the edge."

"Oh, we will!" exclaimed Keiki, forgetting all about the pair of bright red strawberries she would have to part with later in the awe of the moment.

The trees were just barely turning colors, with only a small hue of yellow or orange decorating the leaves. A few mountains peaked in the distance, their purplish tops covered in a powdery snow. Tiki glanced down tentatively. The meadow that the herd called home look absolutely gorgeous from up above. Autumn's final flowers waved in the cool breeze that swept in from the mountains looming in the distance. Tall grass adorned every hilltop and horses dotted the landscape. Bright flashes of bay, gray, black, roan, and white identified each member of the herd. Stargazer sighed contentedly, letting the breeze whisk all her thoughts away.

"It's so beautiful! I don't want to leave this place, ever!"

"Me neither," agreed Marko.

"All the same, we'd best be getting back," Tiki said, reluctantly tearing her eyes away from the beauty around her.

"Of course," nodded Czar, rounding up the foals.

With one last glance at the sunset, they headed back through the woods, across the creek, and into the quiet meadow. A few birds flew overhead and a cricket chirped happily in the brush. Ahead, a tobiano stallion stood alone, seemingly waiting for them.

Suddenly, a wild yell pierced the tranquil silence and shuddered itself through the ears of all present. The single stallion turned quickly to face the oncoming threat, a band of settlers. Humans had been crisscrossing the lands, trying to find a place to set up a bustling town. They had been sighted by the horses several times in the distance and several meetings had been held by the leaders of the herd to discuss the approaching danger.

Seven men appeared on the horizon, all armed with whips, guns, and ropes. Tiki knew they were there for two reasons: For one, to capture horses for plowing and riding. Secondly, to drive the other animals out of "their" territory. The horses froze in fear. A strange silence filled the air and seemed deafening. Czar snorted in sudden anger. He rose up on his hind legs and pawed the air. In the distance, the seven men tried to tie Tretaregon and Kentril to the back of a wagon, drawn by six cattle. The screaming stallions fought back, biting and lashing out ferociously with their hooves. Kentril, Tiki's father, was the first to fall. A short, muscular man brought the barrel of his gun down to hit Kentril across the face. Blood dripped off of the cut created by the painful blow. With a grunt, the stallion tripped to his knees. The man kicked him and rolled him over onto his side. Tying hobbles onto his feet, the grim-faced settler dragged Kentril to the wagon and secured a rope about his neck and muzzle.

Tretaregon rushed to help Kentril. His hind hooves clipped the leader of the settlers, sending him reeling to the ground to nurse a deep wound in his abdomen. Shouting and firing their guns into the air, the intrusive men surrounded Tretaregon and threw ropes at him. He dodged the first and fell headlong into the noose of the next.

"No!" gasped Tiki.

"This is madness! What do these fools think they are doing?" Czar thundered, kicking out his hind legs and bolting after the wagon.

Tiki shot after him and halted in front of him, causing him to skid to a stop. She looked deep into his eyes.

"No, Czar. You cannot go."

"Tiki, they are taking your father! Don't you care? Don't you care that these outsiders, these two-legged menaces, are taking away your father, as well as Tretaregon? What will happen to the herd if Tretaregon and Kentril are gone? We will be leaderless!" shouted Czar angrily. "Step aside!"

"I care for my father more than you think, Czar. What you do not understand is you can't do anything now. It's too late." With tears in her blue eyes, Tiki lifted her head in the direction of the wagon. It rolled quickly away, pulling behind the two stallions. "You can't save them."

"That doesn't stop me from trying."

Czar sidestepped her and burst into a gallop. His anger gave speed to his hooves, and he pounded the ground with shattering force. Tiki again stopped him.

"Listen to me!" she screamed, tears pouring down her face. "They are gone now. If you go after them, you will be caught as well. We need you to lead us, Czar. I need you to lead us. Please."

Czar stared at her for a long time, watching her take ragged breaths between sobs. Her eyes dug deep and split his heart with sympathy. He draped his long neck across her withers and cried with her. She leaned her weight into him. Stargazer approached silently. Tiki opened her eyes, stinging and pink.

"Let's go home," she managed to get out.

Stargazer walked to their favorite knoll of grass and helped a weary Tiki drop to her knees to rest for the night. Or what was left of it. The sun had long set and the star were out. To Czar, however, the stars did not twinkle and glow as brightly as before. They were dull and gray, as if veiled. Czar lay down under a wild apple tree and closed his eyes tightly. The night was cold and dry. Stargazer rested beside Tiki and laid her head comfortingly on the mare's neck.

"Oh, Stargazer. What are we going to do?" Tiki whispered into the darkness. Stargazer did not answer at first; when she did, her voice was very soft.

"Survive."

~Chapter 2~
"Fear"

Tiki blinked in the blazing sunlight. She felt energized and ready for the day. Then, she remembered. It all came back in a flood and she choked back a cry. Stargazer yawned and rolled, all four legs flying in the air. Tiki laughed in spite of her sadness.

"Good morning, Tiki and Stargazer," greeted Arana.

The strawberry roan walked alongside her mother, Sertina. Her eyes were downcast and sad. Sertina said nothing, but only stumbled forward blindly. Tiki heaved to her feet and began cropping grass. A few hours later, all the horses were called together for an important decision.

"Who will be our leader?" questioned Mercury, pacing a hole in the ground.

Silence was his answer. Comanche cleared his throat, catching the attention of all.

"Czar."

Everyone looked from Comanche to Czar and back again.

"Czar," agreed Sertina. "Tretaregon would want it so."

"But Czar is not yet old enough to lead! We should be careful in choosing. Czar is- please take no offense- too soft-hearted to have such responsibility," said cunning Mercury, bowing slightly in Czar's direction.

"Then who would you suggest? Yourself?" snorted Zane.

Mercury bared his teeth at the white colt and Zane backed away, head lowered in fear.

"You say it like it's a bad thing."

"I say it like it's a bad thing because it is a bad thing." Marko shook his mane at Mercury in disgust. Comanche's sons had never taken a liking to Mercury and finally found an opportune time to show it plainly.

"Comanche!" yelled Mercury. "You should teach your sons some respect!" He cantered away muttering, "If I was their leader, they'd see. They'll see." Tiki could glimpse his face contort into an ugly snarl before he was lost from view.

"Czar, you have been chosen to lead our herd. All of our loyalties lie with you," bowed Zane melodramatically, to break the awkward quiet following Mercury's temper tantrum.

Tiki did her best to hide a smile. She moved to Czar's side and groomed his mane, using her teeth to remove any burrs or twigs. His dark forelock rippled in the wind and blew around his face, covering the star on his forehead. Czar bent his head in appreciation and humble acceptance of his task.

"Thank you all for believing in me. I will do my best to live to your expectations of herd leader."

"Good luck, my friend," Tiki whispered in his ear.

The gathering separated and the horses went back to grazing or other various occupations. Czar and Tiki walked side by side through a circle of dandelions. Czar lowered his neck and nibbled the sweet treat, savoring every bite. Tiki stared off into the horizon line, as if looking for something and not finding it.

"Tiki?" Czar hesitated. "Tiki, what are you looking for?"

"I don't rightly know. It feels like I'm missing a piece of myself. My father was all I had. He meant everything to me. And now, he's gone. I've lost him and I don't think I shall ever get him back. Ever since my mother was killed," Tiki said weakly, "I've never really gotten back the feeling of being whole. I always was missing something."

"You have Stargazer. Don't forget her. She'll probably kick you into the forest stream if you do."

Tiki laughed.

"She would! Stargazer is quite a character,

isn't she?"

∎∎∎

Stargazer sighed and abandoned her pile of walnuts. She had been gathering them for many hours and was now bored of the long activity. Tiki and Czar were lying under the walnut tree, talking. She joined them and sang softly under her breath. Czar peered down into a shallow valley on the other side of the hill. Dust gathered as a band of men made their way back to the horses' territory. Stargazer shook with fear and did not move. Tiki began to breathe hard and Czar broke into a sweat as he reared into the sky.

"Run. Run!" commanded Czar, pushing Stargazer to standing.

"Down the hill, Stargazer!" cried Tiki, galloping after Czar.

The roan filly's eyes were filled with terror as she flew across the meadow. Czar gathered the horses together and they pressed on to the edge of the woods. No sooner than the horses had reached their destination, the settlers poured into the meadow. Almost as suddenly as their arrival, they started staking down tents and pounding wooden supports into the hard dirt. Scared and confused, the horses traveled deeper into the woods. They walked for hours, stumbling about in the dying sunlight, tripping over loose stones, bumping into other. Finally, Czar led them inside a large cave.

"It's quite safe. I've been here many a night on my various 'adventures', as I like to call them," Czar laughed lightly, trying to ease up the tension.

No one else laughed, but looked about the cave. A thin stream wove through the back and all the horses drank their fill, tired after the harsh run. Tiki and Zane left the cave to gather ferns for softer bedding than rock and stone. They gathered as many as they could carry and then hurried back to safety. As they reached an open part of the woods, Tiki looked back and could see Tretaregon and Kentril.

Both were tied to heavy metal stakes. They didn't look like the proud Mustang stallions they once were. Tretaregon's bloodbay coat was matted and his tail hacked off. Kentril's mane was tied in small plaits down his neck and his hooves were caked in mud from a day devoted to hauling timber for new houses and shops. A strange look was in their eyes. Tiki closed her eyes. She had seen that look only once before. When the settlers had first been discovered to have entered the plains, Tiki had come face to face with one of the domesticated horses. It couldn't speak. The eyes were dull and glassy. It was completely a dumb animal; no speech could come off its tongue. It had lived so long under human control that it had forgotten how to live like a horse. Tiki had felt pity for the poor old soul, but nothing she said could be comprehended by the animal. Unfortunately for Tretaregon and Kentril, they were beginning to experience that horror firsthand.

Tiki arranged her allotment of ferns on the floor of the cave near Czar. She lay down, still extremely uncomfortable on the hard surface and realizing that a soft bed was just the first luxury she would have to give up during their exile from the meadow. Stargazer plopped down next to her and chewed a mouthful of leaves she had snatched from a short tree just outside the cave. Tiki giggled as the orange leaves hung out of her mouth.

"What?" demanded Stargazer, chewing noisily.

"You look so funny, Stargazer!" laughed Tiki.

"Do not!" retorted the filly.

"Oh, won't you two just go to sleep?" muttered Lara, the daughter of Mercury.

She lay with her chestnut back to her sister, Marta. The two were almost identical looking and loved to play a game in which they pretended to be each other. They were constantly switching identities and confusing the other horses in the herd. Kasandra, their mother, had died the day after they were born due to a serious illness. The two were very close to their father Mercury ever since they were first born. They still missed the presence of a motherly disposition to watch over them and gently raise them.

"Good night, Czar," Tiki called softly.

But Czar did not answer. He stood motionless at the mouth of the cave, watching for predators. The moon gave a faint sliver of pale light, just enough to show Tiki the entire cave. Comanche, Lula, Keiki, Marko, and Zane lay in a circle, each with their heads resting on the back of the horse in front of them. Sertina was sprawled near the stream, her black muzzle gently settled on Arana's neck. Mercury was curled up beside Lara and Marta, and he snored quietly. Stargazer's chest rose and fell in peaceful breaths beside Tiki.

Tiki looked up and watched as the moon made a silver outline around Czar's figure. The shimmering light of the pale moonlight sparkled on his forelock like a crown and created a glistening cape for his withers. His neck was arched proudly in the moonlight and his long, flowing tail spread out behind him. Tiki carefully dropped her head to the ferns on the floor and closed her ocean blue eyes in sleep.

~Chapter 3~
"Thief"

The next morning, Tiki woke early to an aching back and parched mouth. She nudged Stargazer awake, then went to take a drink of water. The cool liquid refreshed her body, and soothed her dry throat. Czar approached from behind and nuzzled her shoulder.

"Tiki, could you please help me for a moment? Outside of the cave?"

"Al-all right. Are you well, Czar?"

"Yes, yes, I am quite well. Let us hurry before the others awaken," he said, hastening out of the cave mouth.

Tiki trotted after him. Czar led her back to the same outlook they had visited the evening that Kentril and Tretaregon were captured. Taking in the view again, Tiki nickered to Czar.

"Czar, what's wrong? You seem troubled."

"I *am* troubled, Tiki. I don't know what to do," he said plainly.

Czar shuddered as he glanced in the direction

of the meadow he had once called home. The anger he wanted to feel burning in his heart against the settlers did not come. Instead, a chill flew up his spine.

"I need to make a decision today," he continued.

"About?"

"Our lives and futures. I know we should leave these regions forever and find a new home where no settlers can take away our freedom. At the same time, I want vengeance. I want the humans to pay for robbing us of our lives. But no! it is not right. The right thing to do is leave. We cannot assault their camps, for we are weak in numbers. They have guns and ropes; we, only our hooves and teeth. These woods and forests will soon be cut down to provide resources for the new town. We are not safe here, Tiki. We must leave," Czar concluded, his eyes never leaving the dirt and stones under his hooves.

Tiki stood in contemplative silence. A bird sang in a tall oak and a few squirrels nearby quarreled over an acorn. She sighed.

"You're right. We do have to leave. And we must do it soon, or not at all!" Tiki exclaimed, staring off into the mountain ranges.

"What do you mean?" Czar questioned curiously.

"Winter is coming on. The snow is falling thick on the mountain tops. It will quickly spread to here. Even the settlers cannot weather it easily, with all their pewter cooking pots and pans. All game will be hiding out for the winter. So should we. Czar, the only obvious thing to do is gather food and find a secure place to winter."

"The safest place is across the mountains in the grasslands of Tekkarui. It is at least a two-week journey. We need to leave tomorrow or the day after. Tiki, please go back to the cave and explain everything to the others. I will begin scoping out provisions for our travels."

Tiki nodded and found her way back to the cave, where she told everyone of Czar's plan. They all agreed unanimously that it was the only way to survive the winter. The grasslands of Tekkarui were rumored to be very fertile and warm. None of them had ever been there, of course, but all were ready to take whatever risks necessary to find out what it was like. Stargazer was the first to approve of the idea. She was willing to follow Tiki and Czar wherever they might go. When Czar returned to the cave, he received a warm welcome and heard excited voices discussing what they were going to do first when they arrived in the grasslands. He gave them another outline of the plan, but his idea of resting peacefully for the rest of the evening was crushed by a sudden bombardment of questions.

Zane wanted to know when they were leaving, Sertina wondered if there were daisies in the grasslands, Comanche announced that he would only go if they could possibly bring a young apple tree, and Mercury fussed over whether or not there was another herd in Tekkarui that he could join. Czar was frustrated and annoyed with the particularity of the herd members.

"Of all the irritating horses in the world, you are the worst, Mercury! No, I don't know if there are other horses. Anyway, you have made a commitment to this herd and you need to fulfill it.

You may not leave without my permission. Now, just, -just go find something useful to do for once," he snorted.

"Czar," scolded Tiki.

Mercury stamped his hoof and slunk away. Tiki shook her mane at Czar in disapproval.

"Was that really necessary?"

Czar ignored her question and continued the discussion over the grasslands. That night, Tiki fell asleep dreaming of sweet grass, soft dirt, and fresh water. She hoped that their new home would be nothing less than plentiful, safe, and most of all, the perfect place for new beginnings.

Stargazer nosed Tiki awake the next morning. She was nearly bouncing out of her coat in excitement.

"Tiki, Tiki, Tiki!" she sang exuberantly. "Czar says we're to leave today. Today!"

"Mmmm….huh?" yawned Tiki, stretching her black and white spotted legs.

"We're leaving today! Czar said for everyone to get up and find provisions! Hurry!" she squeaked, hopping away to tell the rest of the herd.

"I'm coming, I'm coming."

Tiki stood, washed her face in the cool stream, and trotted off to find Czar. He walked to and fro among the trees, searching for acorns and walnuts. A pile of plants, nuts, and produce had already been gathered and placed at the cave entrance.

"Good morning, Czar. Would you like help?" asked Tiki, bumping her muzzle against his muscular shoulder.

"Oh, hello Tiki. Yes, that would be terrific. I need you to do a very risky task. The food needs to be packed into wicker baskets, such as the settlers use. Meaning that you'll need to slip into their camp and steal them," he said hesitantly.

"Steal?"

"Y-yes. About four or five should be enough."

"Well," Tiki started, not wanting to get anywhere near the human settlement, "All right. I'll do it. But Stargazer must stay here. Understood?" she demanded firmly, worried that Stargazer would try to follow her.

"Completely understood, Tiki. You have my word. Now go! It's urgent that we have those baskets so that we can pack them and leave this wretched place. There's a short cut you can take- we took the long way when we first came. The short way is very narrow, but more direct. It should only take you a few minutes to get there on it, if you don't run into trouble. Be careful!"

"Thank you, Czar. I'll go right away. Good-bye!" Tiki called, cantering away.

Her hooves thudded against the forest floor as she sped swiftly through the trees and wild raspberry bushes. Gathering herself, Tiki soared over a log that blocked her path. A small, thin clearing lay on her right. The shortcut Czar had mentioned was very narrow, indeed. Only one horse could pass through at a time and it was very slippery with leaves. Tiki tripped over a rock and fell headlong into a rosebush, thorns and all.

"Ouch!"

She picked herself up, wincing at the half-dozen thorns stuck in each leg. A moan and a groan later, Tiki was stumbling back down the path. Light shone through the branches of the bare trees. Just a yard away, men were hacking at the thick oak trunks with flimsy stone axes. Tiki startled and stepped on a twig harshly.

"Oi! Joey! A mare!" one shouted.

"Shush, Bob, you've scared her!"

"Quick, after her!"

Tiki ignored the thorns in her legs and galloped blindly ahead. The men ran with ropes in hand, throwing them at her clumsily. She dodged them, then stopped short. Four more men were approaching her from the front.

"That's it, mare. Nice and easy. Quiet, now."

"Keep your eye on her. She's got a nasty look, and I wouldn't trust her for a second," warned a mustached man.

Tiki reared and, in the desperation to get away, kicked the two closest men savagely. They crumpled on the ground. The others backed away, hesitant to get any closer. Tiki took her opportunity and dashed through an opening created by the retreating men.

She slowed to a halt as she approached the

growing settlement ahead. Two women walked past where Tiki was hidden, wool skirts swirling about their ankles and feet. They continued to talk and gossip loudly, not noticing the black and white mare trembling behind a tree. She sucked in her breath nervously when the woodcutters she had met entered the settlement, carrying their two fallen comrades.

"Marie! Get Helen and Barty inside! There's a savage horse on the loose!"

"Oh, Martin!" a young woman shrieked, seeing her fiancé bleeding on the ground.

"Martin was kicked by a wild mare in the woods, Jessa."

"I hate those horrible beasts! Why do we have to settle near them? The sight of them simply makes me sick!" Jessa fussed.

Tiki's blood boiled and she ran into the middle of the worried people, not caring that she would most likely be captured. She gave a flying buck and clipped Jessa's shoulder. The woman grabbed a whip and lunged at her, ignoring the screams of her mother. Tiki saw her fast jerking motion. She pinned back her ears and grunted angrily. The mothers anxiously gathered up their children and hurried them inside various tents. Jessa's mother dragged her into a big blue canvas tent. Tiki let out a fierce whinny and frightened the rest of the people into hiding.

She waited another minute, until she was sure it was safe, before making a quick dash for a heap of supplies. All matter of cooking tools were mounded together on the ground. Pots, pans, spoons, and dishes were all nosed aside as Tiki searched through the pile. Finally, she spotted baskets tied to each other with thick twine. Not having time to bite loose five from the bunch of ten baskets, Tiki snatched them all up and galloped back to the edge of the woods.

While she ran, she couldn't help but notice two horses, side by side, straining to pull a heavy plow. Kentril's tobiano coat was slick with sweat and Tretaregon gasped for every breath. Tiki winced when she heard the sharp cracking of a whip and the moan of a horse in pain. She entered the woods and made the slow and tiring climb back to the cave. Czar was waiting for her at the entrance with Stargazer pacing worriedly beside him.

"Tiki! Oh, I was so anxious! Did you get through all right?" the filly exclaimed, leaping forward to meet her.

"Not quite, Stargazer. I met a band of men in the woods. They were chopping down trees. I stepped on a stick and they saw me. When they tried to catch me, I-I attacked them. I ran to the settlement and they warned the people. A young female tried to whip me and I kicked her. I also saw Tretaregon and my father slaving in a field, pulling a metal object that looked terribly heavy. I do wish we had time to free them before we leave," said Tiki wistfully.

"You *attacked* them?" Czar asked, surprise in his voice.

"It was that or be captured."

She dropped her burden for Czar to inspect and let Stargazer drag her into the cave to rest.

"Czar says that we're not leaving until *tomorrow*," whined Stargazer.

"I suppose we're too behind schedule with preparations to leave just yet."

"In that case, I'm going to help Czar until my bones break. Do you think that would help us leave today? I really want to go now. All this waiting is getting on my nerves!"

Tiki laughed. "Be patient, dear. We'll leave soon enough. But you're right; we do need to help speed up the packing process. Where's Czar? There must be loads to do!"

■■

Hours of hard work later, Tiki placed her head on the soft fern leaves that covered a small portion of the cave. Closing her eyes, she fell into a deep sleep, resting her heart and mind. Stargazer collapsed next to her but did not sleep so easily. She lay there for a very long time, her mind wandering from thought to dream and back again. Scrambling to her feet, Stargazer stepped outside the cave to watch the sun rising back into the sky. A rabbit hopped out of a bush, happily munching a wildflower.

"Why, hello! It's a rabbit! Aren't you just the cutest thing?" she giggled to herself.

"Excuse me, but I can hear and think well enough for myself, thanks. As for cute, I don't have a clue as to what you're hinting at," the rabbit burst out impudently.

"Oh. Sorry, sir," Stargazer apologized, surprised at the sudden speech of the tiny animal.

He fluffed up his white fur, seeming offended, and hopped back inside his bush. Stargazer stared after him. She turned and found Czar and Tiki smiling at her.

"Good morning!" she said cheerfully.

"Ah, you are all ready to leave, I see." Czar laughed. "I will wake the others. We must begin our long trek into the mountains today. Please pile the food together," he requested, trotting to the cave mouth.

"Yes, Czar," Tiki and Stargazer chorused.

They nosed the baskets into a neat stack. Keiki came out to them, her silvery-gray mane flowing in the slight breeze. She sighed contentedly as she ate a wild raspberry off a bush. The crimson juice dripped off her rosy muzzle and onto the leaves under her hooves.

"Oops," she laughed, accidentally knocking a berry onto the ground.

She gobbled it up and turned to help Tiki nudge an especially large basket full of freshly picked apples. Czar returned with the rest of the herd. He gave out his various orders and began tying baskets onto the shoulders of the stronger horses. It was hard, using a muzzle instead of human fingers to do a delicate job of knotting rope.

"Tiki! Could you help me?" gasped Stargazer, trying to push a tiny basket of nuts on top of Keiki.

"Of course, Stargazer!"

Tiki strode over to help the fillies. Nosing the basket onto Keiki's withers, Tiki let Stargazer use her teeth to tie a triple knot in the ropes. Keiki reached her head around and tugged on the basket. It stayed snuggly atop her shoulders.

Once all the horses were ready, Czar took his

place at the front of the herd. He had arranged the procession so that the foals were inside a protective ring created by the adults. They traveled quickly through the woods, only stopping once or twice to refresh themselves with water and bits of food from their baskets. Czar carefully rationed the provisions to help make them last as long as they could.

"Forward!"

"Come on, Arana!" giggled Keiki, bumping into her friend.

Arana stood silent in the center of the path, blocking Keiki off from the rest of the group. She woke from her apparent daydream and trotted ahead.

~Chapter 4~
"Destruction"

Tiki dropped to her knees, sweaty mane dragging in the dirt. They had marched long into the night and on into the morning, not stopping until the sun had again reached the center of the sky. Stargazer sprawled out next to her, breathing hard.

"I-," she moaned, "I can't m-move."

"I know how you feel, Stargazer. My legs are limp and exhausted. Let's rest now."

Czar made sure everyone was comfortable lying in bushes and under low trees. He wanted to stay hidden all the rest of the day before they moved again. The least information about their journey and small numbers, the better they would fare. Running into danger in the mountains was not a light subject.

Czar tucked his legs under his body and stretched his head out towards Tiki. He nickered quietly to her and Tiki smiled as she slept. Stargazer was snoring peacefully, her resting hooves caked in dried mud from the long journey in the woods. Czar looked around at their surroundings and sighed. The horses were close to exiting the shelter of the trees and entering the exposure of the mountain ranges. They would be spending most of the remaining trip out in the open mountains. In these particular mountains, trees were rare and the whole range was unsheltered from rain and snow.

"We'll need a lot of luck to get across those without being seen by wolves," muttered Czar, closing his eyes.

Tiki groaned as Czar shook her awake that night. A few rays of moonlight drifted through the leaves, setting a tranquil mood to the darkness.

"Please help me with the others," yawned Czar, eyes tired and still misty with sleep.

"All right."

Tiki had a difficult time waking and gathering the horses back into formation. They pressed on again, stumbling around in the dark until the sun climbed into the sky and lit up the forest. Tiki was distracting the younger colts and fillies with jokes and made-up stories she invented along the way. She had the full attention of all the foals as she told them about magical worlds and the creatures that lived there.

"And so," Tiki concluded, "Marsilusa never again ventured within ten feet of a bird without turning to ice temporarily."

"I liked that one. Marsilusa deserved the curse that Karte put on her. She was absolutely wicked!" exclaimed Stargazer.

"Well, *I* feel sorry for *Geikdna*! His daughter was turned into a fish and his son was locked up in a dungeon for the last twenty-seven years of his life!" Keiki pouted, drooping her bottom lip.

"I certainly don't like Karte. He had no reason to curse Marsilusa in the first place! Yes, she did imprison Geikdna's son, and turn his daughter into a fish, and kill all the kings in the tournament by poisoning them, and make the entire kingdom into a desert, but other than that, all she accomplished was try to take over the world!" said Zane, much annoyed that his favorite heroine was being bashed.

Tiki exchanged a quick smile with Czar, then tuned back into the chatter that followed her animated storytelling.

"And she very nearly succeeded! If Karte hadn't stopped her, she would be ruling the world at this exact moment!" cried Tiki dramatically.

The foals' eyes widened.

"That was a-a-a *true* story? There really is magic?" questioned Stargazer.

"Where do I find magic?" pleaded Keiki, dancing alongside Tiki.

"I need magic better than any of you. I *have* to turn Marta into a wild boar," announced Lara, "or I will *die!*"

"No, Stargazer, I don't believe there is magic. That's just a story that I made up along the way while we were walking."

Their ears drooped sadly.

"Even if there was magic, Keiki, I really don't know where to find it! I'd start by looking around you. Sometimes a forest or lake can be so beautiful that you might say it is magical. And Lara," Tiki paused to laugh, "I think Marta would love you all the more if you did *not* turn her into a wild boar. Am I correct?"

Tiki gasped and turned her head from side to side. They were out of the forest and the shade of the trees, and into the chilly mountain air. The ground was hard and stony everywhere she looked.

"Tiki, the valley!"

She peered down the mountainside. There was their old home, still the same rolling hills and scattered trees. Replacing the gentle grasses and flowers, freshly plowed fields covered the landscape. Numerous wooden structures decorated every hilltop and valley. Thick smoke rose from uncountable cook fires, blanketing the growing town. Men were chopping down trees in every direction. Some split the logs into boards and sanded them smooth. A couple of older boys were helping to clear a lot by burning the tall grass. The fire would spread a few inches out of line, and a boy would stomp out the unwanted flame. Soon, the strong aroma of burning grass and leaves reached the nostrils of the horses. Tiki sniffed back a tear.

"They are ruining our home."

"It is no longer our home, Tiki."

Czar stood behind her, calm and reassuring. All the foals were back in the procession and already trotting ahead. Tiki choked back a sob and buried her head in Czar's shoulder. He returned her embrace and let a few of his own tears slide loose.

"Oh, Tiki! I know how much it hurts to leave. But we cannot fight for our home, such as they can. We must learn to move on, to find another dream to chase. You told me you wanted to find that missing sense of wholeness. This journey may just fulfill that dream. Forget the past and enjoy the future, Tiki. And now, let's hurry! The grasslands of Tekkarui are calling! Away we go!"

■■■

Stargazer danced around Tiki excitedly.

"What's going on, Stargazer?"

"I have something for you!"

"Dandelions! Wherever did you find them?" squealed Tiki, joining in on her excitement.

"Czar found them. He told me you were upset and asked if there was anything you would want. I said you loved dandelions, and he left Mercury in charge so he could search for some. He must have been really desperate to have *him* be in charge. Here, take them."

"Oh, thank you, Stargazer!"

Tiki gave the filly a few of her flowers and then set off to find Czar. She found him speaking to Comanche in a light tone. Seeing him laughing was a surprise for Tiki. Ever since Tretaregon and Kentril's capture, he had been grave and thoughtful. Tiki loved his advice, but missed his cheery self. Comanche saw Tiki and smiled understandingly. He nodded his head to Czar and trotted away.

"Czar!"

"Hello, Tiki! How are you feeling?" he laughed.

"Better now. Stargazer gave me the

dandelions from you. Thank you, Czar. It really cheered me up, especially after seeing the meadow in ruins."

"I'm glad. We should start moving again. Sertina swears that when her bones ache, snow is coming. Redantre agrees that the weather is beginning to change for the worst. He is a smart young foal."

"Yes, he is," agreed Tiki.

"I think we should feed the herd and start on our way. Soon enough, night traveling will no longer be safe, even a group, no matter how large. Wolves and cougars will be roaming these parts at night, so the earlier we start, the farther we can journey before it becomes dangerous."

Tiki and Czar raced each other along the cliff's edge, enjoying the exhilarating thrill of a race. They arrived back to find confusion everywhere. The foals were munching contently on their rations, but the adults argued and bickered amongst themselves.

"I saw it all, Lula. You took four times as many thistles as portioned. We ought to make you go without any more for the rest of the journey!" shouted Mercury, tugging a mouthful from the mare.

"Are you trying to starve us all by stuffing your muzzle with nuts, Comanche? Leave some for the rest of us!" Sertina demanded, nipping the stallion's gray shoulder.

Comanche dropped the nut he was cracking and yelped in pain. He turned and kicked his hind legs at Sertina. The blow missed the mare and instead overturned a basket of dried grass.

"Now look at what you've done!" the mare cried triumphantly.

"It was *your* fault!" retorted Comanche, nosing the food back into the basket.

"What is going on here?" thundered Czar, stomping his hoof on the hard rock cliff.

He immediately had the attention of all. The troublemaking horses tried to not look guilty but failed.

"Get ahold of yourselves! You're fighting like human children! Mercury, you are a stallion, not a misbehaving colt! Lula had her allotted amount. Give back her thistles and *apologize*. I trusted you with the herd a few minutes ago so I could run an errand and this is what I come back to. Sertina, I am most displeased with your behavior. I'm counting on you to be a good example for our young mares and fillies. Now, finish up your *normal* rations and get into line. We need to get moving before nightfall. Prowling predators will soon be upon us and we cannot stop for long."

The foals hurriedly crammed their mouths with the last crumbs of food and skipped into line. Both of the mares were humbled greatly by Czar and stood quietly in their designated positions. Comanche helped Tiki and Czar load the horses with baskets. Mercury stormed about furiously, running blindly back and forth to push the remaining baskets together in a pile. In his blundering, he knocked over a basketful of thistles. Looking quickly about, Mercury discovered that no one had seen the spillage. He nosed the basket and fallen thistles over the cliff, then went along his business like nothing had happened.

~Chapter 5~
"Fight"

The horses walked and trotted the entire night, never coming across any other animal but rabbits. None of them had noticed the absence of the thistle basket, much to the relief of Mercury. He was still angry with Czar for calling him out in front of the entire herd. Determined to make the leading stallion pay, he again 'accidentally' knocked another basket of wild corn. The basket of corn was only half-filled, but the loss would cut rations down. When the horses had stopped under an outcropping of rock to spend the remainder of the morning in sleep, Tiki found Czar. Her tone was anxious and immediately worried Czar.

"Czar, I was giving out portions of food and found that we have two baskets less than two days ago. That doesn't seem right."

"No, it doesn't, Tiki. I'll look into it. We may have finished some. What is missing?"

"Thistles and wild corn."

"Just last afternoon, Lula was eating thistles.

There was still plenty in the basket. Maybe it was packed in a different basket?"

"I don't believe that would be the case. And I gave Stargazer some of my unfinished corn ration during the night trek. I hadn't gotten mine until after everyone else did. It was half-full then. Czar, I'm worried. What if we don't have enough food to last the entire journey?"

"We'll be fine, Tiki. I will inspect what we have left and if we have to cut down portions, then that's what we'll do. It's only a little food missing," consoled Czar. "Now let's get some sleep before the next hike. Each day, we travel even deeper into the mountain range. The grasslands will be visible soon."

Tiki leaned onto Czar as they walked back to the herd. A heavy slumber overtook her and dreams flew about her mind. She flashed back to a fateful day, many years before.

A black Mustang mare grazed peacefully with a paint filly at her side. The scream of a cougar echoed through the hills as he raced at the unprotected pair. He rose on his hind paws and swiped at the panicking mare. She fought back as best she could, using her hoofs and trying to stay between the filly and the growling monster. The claws of the huge cat tore deep into her shoulder and pierced her quickly beating heart. Jestia, the mare, gave one final shriek and collapsed to the ground in a pool of fresh blood. The filly shouted in agony and rushed full gallop to her mother's side.

"Mother! Mother, no!"

"Tiki! Get away! Run!" *trumpeted Kentril, charging at the cougar.*

"Tiki? Tiki!"

"Mother! Mother, no!"

"What?" asked a confused Stargazer.

"Stargazer? Oh, thank goodness. It was so real," shuddered Tiki, remembering the dream.

"Czar wants you. We're about to leave."

"Thank you."

Tiki stood and trotted to where Czar was frowning at the pile of wicker baskets containing the food.

"Yes, Czar?"

"Good morning, Tiki," he said shortly.

"Is-is everything all right?"

"No," Czar laughed bitterly. "No, everything's not okay. The apples and nuts are gone."

"*All* the apples and nuts?"

"All the apples and nuts," echoed Czar.

Tiki shook her mane indignantly. She helped Czar dole out noticeably smaller helpings to the herd, realizing that if they didn't cover more ground in less time, the food would soon run out. At the same time, the more energy that the herd needed, the more food they would require to stay healthy. After eating, Czar led the horses on again. Tiki traded jokes with the foals to keep their minds off the longer journey Czar was pushing them through. The terrain steadily grew worse, as did the weather. A light rain dripped through the clouds and splattered onto shivering coats. Rocks were slippery and Tiki cautioned the foals to carefully eye their footings. Once, Zane's hooves skidded across a flat rock and he crashed against

Mercury. The angry stallion spun around so fast, Tiki got whiplash from observing his movements.

"Watch it! Move off, colt," he growled, stamping his hoof.

"Sorry, sir. I promise I di,"

"*Quiet!*" yelled Mercury, slamming into the colt and sending him reeling backwards.

Czar hadn't seen the exchange and still trotted on ahead. Lula bent her head and Comanche set his jaw as he approached Mercury.

"Get away from my son! Now," demanded Comanche.

He stared Mercury down until the reprimanded stallion snorted carelessly and rushed back into place. Lara was silent for once and Marta looked like she might cry. Tiki nuzzled the two chestnuts and tried to lift their heavy hearts. They were grateful for her compassion, but continued to be crushed by the strange behavior of their father. Zane was sniffling behind Tiki and she turned to him.

"Zane!" she exclaimed.

"I'm all right, Tiki. I'll be fine."

A thick stream of blood poured down his white coat from his withers. One glance told Tiki that he wasn't all right. When Mercury had pushed Zane, the colt had fallen and struck his back on a sharp rock, slicing the skin open.

"No, you won't. I'm telling Czar," insisted Tiki.

But she didn't have to move a step. Czar was already cantering over. He had seen the blood and stopped the herd instantly.

"What happened, Zane?"

"Well, I, um," began the white colt.

His eyes darted about and finally came to rest on Mercury. The stallion was staring furiously at him. Mercury mouthed to him, *'One word out of turn, and you're dead. I've got my eye on you'.* Zane started over, scared by the threat that only he had seen.

"I slipped on the wet ground and fell on top of a sharp rock. It cut my back open," he lied.

Czar spent a few minutes inspecting the

wound. He crushed healing herbs under his hoof and applied them to Zane's blood-stained coat. Zane announced that he would be fine to walk again, and the herd started off.

•••

The horses slowed as the rain intensified. A slight rise in terrain forced them out of a trot for the rest of the journey. Czar stopped the herd on a flat cliff. There was plenty of room for all the horses to rest. All the horses lay down in a snug circle, flanks touching the horses on either side. Their heads were bent tightly towards their chests. Mercury snickered and lay off by himself. Lara came to his side but he turned his back on her. She dragged herself away and laid down next to Marta, tears dripping down her muzzle. Czar tucked his knees under his stomach next to Tiki. Stargazer was already asleep on Tiki's withers. Her blue roan coat was soaked and muddy, created by the rain being absorbed into the dirt already dusted on her delicate body.

"We leave at sunrise," said Czar, muffling a yawn. "I know you're all tired. The sooner we start, the quicker we will reach the grasslands."

"If they even exist," Sertina mumbled under her breath.

Redantre shot her a silencing look and turned back to Keiki. The two had grown closer in friendship, much to Keiki's liking. He was very intelligent about wildlife outside their own kinds, which Keiki was very interested in. Czar cocked his head at Sertina and she seemed to sink into the ground under his gaze.

"I want to say something to you all before we sleep. That goes for you, too, Mercury," added Czar, voice rising so that Mercury could hear. "I have witnessed some of the behavior that has been going on in our herd. I am very disappointed in a few of you." He glanced around the group, eyes resting on a couple of horses and passing over others. Clearing his throat, he continued. "A herd survives when they work together. We are not working together. Our food is running low. Those who do not wish to cooperate may as well lose the privilege of being a member of this herd. Do you all understand? You chose me as a leader. Will you or will you not accept and obey my rules? Will you follow me?"

"I will."

Tiki's blue eyes shone in the darkness as she lifted her voice.

"I always have and always shall," announced Comanche. "As well as my family.

Lula, Keiki, Marko, and Zane all nodded in agreement.

"Yes. I will," said Arana. Sertina echoed her statement quietly.

Each horse quickly spoke up with their decision to cooperate and follow Czar's lead without complaint. Except Mercury. Everyone waited in dreadful silence. A bitter laugh cut through the air, piercing the tranquil night.

"Me? Oh, but of course, Czar! I will *always* be by your side, as a *faithful* citizen of the herd. Really? I don't care about what happens to any of you! You'll all die out here, anyways. Czar will only prolong your fate and make your pain continue for as long as he can. Do you actually think *he* worries about you? With that Tiki whispering straight into his narrow brain, do you really think he sees or hears anything else? All she encourages is for him to keep on tyrannizing over us."

Tiki laid her ears flat against her neck and tensed her muscles. Czar put a gentle muzzle on her shoulder, stopping her from doing anything rash. But Tiki was enraged with Mercury and her voice showed it plainly.

"Mercury, since you obviously have quite a dislike for me and Czar, why don't you just leave? I certainly won't miss your glares and stares. Your daughters are safe with Sertina, Lula, and I. Please just go and save our sanity," she hissed through clenched teeth.

"Oh, I see it all so clearly now! You want me to leave! You've been making me angry on purpose, to show me as the moody, stupid horse. Well then! I believe I'll stay!"

Czar was silent throughout the whole exchange. He finally raised his head and locked eyes with Mercury.

"Leave."

"Excuse me?"

"I said *leave!* You wanted to leave once before. I told you not without permission could you leave. Now you are permitted. Just get out of the herd and don't come back!" shouted Czar, jumping to his feet.

"Fine, Czar. Nothing to get excited about yet. You'll all have your party as soon as I'm gone. Give me provisions and I'll leave more or less peacefully."

Tiki hurriedly gave Mercury food and water. He didn't thank her. He just walked away, not even bothering to say good-bye to his daughters. Lara choked and hid her face. Marta stared after her father, body shaking with sobs. Sertina nickered to her and the filly set her head on the mare's thick neck. Mercury turned and called over his shoulder.

"Been wondering why you're running low on food? I've thrown thistles, wild corn, apples, and nuts over the edge of the cliff. I poked holes in the baskets and even fed birds with the foals' rations if they weren't paying attention. Have fun starving in the mountains!" he laughed.

Mercury gathered himself, jumped over a jagged rock, and vanished into the twilight.

~Chapter 6~
"Snow"

Tiki woke early to the sounds of soft weeping. Lara stood at the edge of the cliff, sobbing her heart out. Hearing Tiki's approach, the chestnut filly turned and ran to the older mare.

"H-how could he leave u-us?" she hiccupped.

"I don't know. From my point of view, it seems like his heart was so bitter that he just snapped. I don't understand life, Lara. It was all flowers and blue skies when I was a yearling. Now it's thorns and black clouds. I think we all need a little sun right now."

Tiki and Lara rejoined the herd. Each horse only got a few flakes of dried grass, half a peach, two nuts, and a handful of leaves. Breakfast was short and the herd was on their way very soon after sunrise. The weather was gentle, with a soft breeze coming from the north and the warm sun beating down on their backs. For the most part, silence reigned in the mountains. Stargazer would occasionally sing a silly song that reminded the horses of the funny memories they had from their old home. Tiki trotted ahead and stayed close by Czar's side for the rest of the day. They laid out plans for life in the grasslands and decided important guidelines for the herd to live by. As the day was ending, Stargazer gave an excited shout.

"Snow!"

Sure enough, snowflakes swirled lightly around the horses. They stuck in the blue roan filly's eyelashes and she giggled.

"This means winter is coming on. We must press on!" cried Czar.

"Press on!" echoed the other horses.

Trotting through the night was difficult, as the only light to guide them on was from the stars and the moon. Clouds rolled across the sky and quenched the faint glow of light. Czar stopped the herd for a rest when it was too dangerous to travel. A wolf howled at the hidden moon and the foals trembled in fear. Czar stood and paced to and fro, listening for more wolves. Satisfied with the absence of the beasts, he lay back down. While Czar regained some needed sleep, Tiki stayed awake to keep watch. All was tranquil and still. She smiled as the clouds slid away into the night, revealing the twinkling stars. The snow was falling steadily and covering the rocks with its powdery substance. Tiki was reminded of the days when she was a yearling.

"What is it, Mother? It's so cold!" squealed Tiki.

"This is snow, Tiki. Snow falls in the winter. Soon, the whole meadow will be deeply covered in it!" exclaimed Jestia.

The black and white filly leapt through the air and plunged back down into a pile of snow.

Tiki shook herself from the dream. The sun was climbing up the sky and pushing the moon back to its hiding place. Czar snored beside her, though Tiki could not see him in the faint light. Everything was covered in snow, from the mountain peaks to the horses themselves.

"Czar! Czar, wake up!"

The coat of the stallion was barely visible under all the snow. He shook it off and struggled to his feet. For the first time, Tiki noticed how thin he was. Czar's ribs were showing through his coat and his backbone was more visible than it should've been.

"You're so thin, Czar! Here, take some of my fruit!"

"No, Tiki. You need to keep up your strength," he refused.

"But-,"

"Tiki. Eat your fruit and I'll have mine. Really, I'm fine."

"All right."

Stargazer yawned and scarfed down her food. She, too, looked skinny and worn. The other horses finished their breakfasts and Czar led them on again. Trekking through snow was a harder experience than they had expected. Covering ground at a fast trot was not possible, as the foals constantly tripped in the deep blanket of white. Czar and Comanche broke a path before the herd, shoving snow into high walls on either side. Tiki guided the horses forward and in this fashion, they were able to gain lost ground. In flat places, a bright canter was acceptable. For the rockier hills, a trot served their purposes well. A few times, Stargazer stumbled and fell. She had a difficult time getting up again, which worried Tiki immensely.

"Stargazer, are you *sure* you're all right? I can carry you on my back if you are too tired to walk," offered Tiki.

"Of course I'm all right! I can walk," insisted Stargazer.

Tiki kept an eye on the filly for the next few minutes. Stargazer proved that she was fine, and Tiki relaxed slightly. Czar and Comanche dropped back into line with the herd. They had cleared a mile of snow. Tiki brushed snow off Czar's back. He was breathing hard and sweating from the tough task.

"When we reach the point where Comanche and I stopped clearing snow, we'll stop for the day," he gasped.

The remainder of the journey was easy and the horses rested for the night in peace. Waking early, Tiki watched Stargazer rest. More than twice, the yearling filly coughed, her body trembling. Stargazer's muscles were growing but her weight diminished quickly. Her eyes were pink and bloodshot. Tiki dug into the basket of herbs and hastily stomped a pasty substance out of the greenery to spread around the filly's eyes. After applying the salve, Tiki woke Czar.

"Czar, I'm scared. Stargazer is very sick."

"I'll give her extra food today and we'll see if that will help," reassured Czar.

"But we have no extra! All we have is rations for another two days. Unless we cut down the daily portions, the food won't hold on long enough."

"Stargazer can have my ration."

"Then you'll be hungry!"

"Tiki, please stop worrying. We'll make it! I promise."

Stargazer was wakened only just before the horses started off, to allow her more rest. She coughed and the sound made Tiki sick with anxiety. Barely knowing what was happening around her, Stargazer ate her ration, as well as Czar's. Had she known that it was more than usual, she would have refused the food. Redantre helped Marko lift Stargazer onto Tiki's back. The filly was as light as a feather, and Tiki had no struggle carrying her weight across her withers. Czar slipped a few times, becoming weaker and weaker with each passing hour. Stargazer slept the whole day and on into the night, waking in the late morning when the daily journey was already far under way.

"Tiki," she said, stopping her sentence to cough hoarsely, "Y-you need a rest from bearing me. Let me walk."

"No, Stargazer. You are not well. Besides, carrying you is like having an inch of snow on my back!"

Stargazer weakly gave in, letting Tiki continue to carry her. Exhausted, Czar halted the horses well after nightfall.

"Sleep while you can. Stay near each other to keep warm," was all he could manage to get out.

Czar was asleep before Tiki could even lower to the ground to let Stargazer slide off. The filly's cough was slowly getting less harsh and Tiki slept well, knowing Stargazer was on her way to recovery. Czar was sluggish the next day, stumbling weakly about. Tiki stopped the herd earlier than usual to give him a break. He drifted in and out of sleep. A fever came upon him and his sweat chilled his bones. Tiki stood over him to provide a little shelter from the elements. Czar slipped into unconsciousness, wandering in a world of nightmares and monsters.

"He won't last long like this," panicked Sertina.

"Do we have *any* food he can have?" begged Tiki.

"I'm afraid not. Let's all give him bits of our own rations," proposed Comanche, digging into the food baskets.

The horses all agreed with him and immediately gave up scraps of grass and fruits. Tiki insisted that Stargazer keep her food to maintain her recovery, though the kind-hearted foal pleaded with her.

"But Tiki! Czar could *die!*"

"And so could you!" argued Tiki.

"Bu-,"

"No. Eat up and go to sleep. I need to decide what to do."

~Chapter 7~
"Alone"

Tiki paced long into the night, thinking. The herd could still move forward if they would somehow be able to bear Czar. Food was too scarce to stay and the mountain provided little to no shelter. She searched through the remaining supplies and sighed. Nothing but a small bit of food. Peering over the cliff's edge, she spied a smooth path down the mountainside.

She lay down next to Stargazer. Czar was resting his head limply on a smooth rock, chest rising and falling. Comanche's family huddled together against the cold. Lara and Marta curled up, their chestnut coats dusted with snow. They were lonely and upset without Mercury. He had crushed their young hearts and, in his actions, showed them a glimpse of the world outside the carefree life of a foal.

Redantre had his muzzle under his leg, letting the warm breath from his nostrils heat and melt the snow beneath him. Arana was leaning on her mother, who snored gently.

Stargazer awoke before the rest of the herd. She stood carefully, still weak from sickness. Nosing Tiki, she woke the paint mare.

"Morning!"

"Hello, Stargazer. What are you doing up at this time in the morning?" groaned Tiki.

"It's really not that early. The sun has been up for a minute or two," figured Stargazer.

"My point exactly," the mare yawned.

"Get up, get up!" giggled Stargazer.

Tiki playfully nudged her away and clambered to her feet, feeling exhausted and spent. Waking the rest of the herd, she explained her discovery of the path down the mountain and asked Comanche to carry Czar.

"Let's hurry before the clouds give any more snow!" exclaimed Keiki, shivering.

Zane walked ahead with Tiki. Comanche followed them with Czar over his withers. Tiki called for a trot as the land evened out. Stargazer became tired after only a few minutes of trotting, so Redantre lay down and let her climb aboard his back. He scrambled to his feet and caught up with the herd.

The youthful stallion carried her with ease and told the filly jokes until she cried from laughter. A few of the foals grew antsy and longed to run across grassy meadows and splash in cool streams. Sertina contented them with the idea that within a couple of days, they would do just that. Tiki allowed the herd to speed up to a canter, but made sure Comanche and Redantre were up to the task. The two stallions were hardly winded by the change in pace and they kept it up for a long time.

"Father, tell us again of the old squirrel who used to drop acorns on Uncle Dekku!" giggled Keiki.

"Not again!" groaned the other foals collectively.

Keiki had asked for the story numerous times during the entirety of the day.

"I think we'll wait a bit on that one, Keiki," chuckled Comanche, shaking his head.

"We can slow to a walk now," announced Tiki.

The only sounds that the horses could hear was the thudding of bare hooves on stone and the beating of their hearts. Czar muttered in his sleep, which quite worried Tiki. She stayed close by his side and made sure he was comfortable.

"Tiki, I can still save them! Let me through!" moaned Czar, shaking with fever.

His breath came in gasps and he began to cough up blood.

"Czar! Stay with me, Czar!"

"Tiki," Comanche hesitated.

"What should I do, Comanche? He's dying! There's nothing I can do for him anymore. We have barely enough food to keep the breath in our own lungs and Czar….won't….wake….up!" she hiccupped.

"Easy now, easy! Stop the herd at nightfall and we'll discuss what step is next. We *will* make it, as will Czar."

"You sound so sure. How can you see past

reality?" she sniffed.

"I can't. I just know he'll make it. Czar's a fighter. He'll pull through."

Tiki brought the pace up to a canter again, trying to gain as much ground as they could before the sun dropped from the sky. A ring of tall rocks towered above the horses. They cautiously entered the circle and found it to be completely safe.

"We will stay here for the night."

Comanche lay down to unload Czar. Stargazer slipped sleepily from Redantre's withers and found a place to sleep. The horses settled down, hungry and malnourished, to listen to Tiki.

"Friends," she started. "I do not know how much longer this journey may take. We have no food left for tomorrow. It has held out this far, but now has come to an end. What do we do?"

"Send a strong horse out before us to find food and any signs of the grasslands," proposed Sertina.

"Who? Who will go?" asked Lula.

The horses looked around at each other, expectantly. All at once, their gazes fell on Tiki.

"Tiki could go," said Keiki slowly. "She is still much healthier than the rest of us and has a strong will to reach our destination."

"Who would lead the herd if I go?"

"Comanche," the other horses replied in unison.

"I believe we can call this meeting adjourned, then!" yawned Tiki, lying down and preparing her mind for the task ahead.

∎∎

Tiki opened her eyes just as the sun climbed into the heavens. Getting to her feet, she woke Stargazer. The filly stretched and moaned tiredly.

"Good morning, Stargazer. I'm leaving now."

"Why can't I come with you?" she grumped.

"Because you're not well yet!"

"My cough is better!"

Tiki sighed.

"No. I'll be back very soon," she assured.

"Promise?"

"Promise."

Stargazer watched reluctantly as Tiki trotted away. Comanche let the horses rest for a while longer to regain strength for their climb.

"Everyone up!"

Stargazer stood solemnly, her eyes following the shrinking black and white speck steadily descending the peak.

"Come on, Stargazer! You're holding us back," grumbled Arana.

. . . .

Tiki slowly made her way over sharp rocks and steep drop-offs. She was traveling the most difficult part of the mountains. A sudden cliff stopped her short in her tracks.

"Now what?"

As if in answer to her question, a large eagle swooped past her head and flew between two large boulders. Tiki followed him and he led her down a steep incline. Panting, she entered a flat stretch of dirt. A thin trickle of water dripped off of a rock and Tiki drank thirstily.

"Hmmm...might as well get past this part of the land before night. I'll gallop for a while."

Tiki broke to a trot and let herself into a canter. After a few strides, she leapt into a ground-eating gallop. Dust gathered behind her and clouded the air. She peered ahead and let her pace slacken. A wall of stones had slid off an overhang of rock and blocked her path. Snorting, Tiki rocked back on her haunches and propelled powerfully over the wall. She increased her speed, stretching out her legs and feeling the wind ripple through her mane. Only a few hundred feet lay between her and the next stretch of mountainous terrain. The pain of emptiness in her stomach was unbearable and her legs ached horribly. A single tree stood alone, its leaves still intact and the bark a deep brown. Tiki pushed her weariness to the back of her thoughts and raced to it. She collapsed beneath it, gasping for breath.

Reaching her muzzle up, she plucked a leaf from the branches and tasted it. The leaf was hard and bitter, but it was nourishing nonetheless. Tiki ate as much as she could hold and then closed her eyes in slumber.

~Chapter 8~
"Wolves"

"Forward!" shouted Comanche, struggling valiantly on.

Stargazer was jerked about on his back and tried to keep her balance. The ground they were treading was hard to travel and the horses were weak from hunger. Czar had awakened and was fed with the last of the food. He drifted back to sleep, his fever rising with the incline of terrain. Redantre stumbled and fell, scraping open his knees. Blood ran down his hooves and pooled around them.

"Redantre! Are you all right?" called Zane.

"I-I think so. We can't stop now. Let's keep moving," groaned Redantre, through clenched teeth.

Lula pressed her strong black back against a rock and pushed it out of the way. It tumbled off the cliff and broke in two at the bottom.

"Ahh!" Sertina screamed in pain. Her hoof had

gotten caught in a hole and twisted. She fell on her side and nuzzled her sore foot.

"Everyone, go on ahead. I'll get Sertina," called Marko, trotting to the mare's side.

"Thank you," she whispered.

Marko examined the hoof, completely bruised and swelling about the fetlock. He knelt down and Sertina miserably clambered on. They quickly caught up with the herd.

Tiki wheezed and nipped her sides. The leaves she had devoured were churning in her stomach and making her sick.

"Ohhhh," she moaned, rolling back and forth to stop the pain.

The sun was setting and shooting rays of light across the sky. Tiki gave a harsh kick against the tree. Some of the bark splintered and landed at her feet. She ate the sap that flowed on the underside of the bark. The sticky sap soothed her stomach and made her sleepy. Tiki folded her knees and lay down. Yawning, she decided to rise earlier than usual the next morning to cover more ground.

Czar's condition worsened. His cough grew sharper and tore at his throat. Waking only once every few hours, he barely ate. Stargazer was getting stronger and helped Comanche lead the herd. Her infectious spirit lifted everyone's hopes of seeing the grasslands.

"Tiki will find them! If anyone can do it, Tiki can!" she said firmly.

"We have no food. We're going to die!" despaired Arana.

"It's not over yet!" declared Stargazer, fighting to pull her small frame over a rock.

Comanche and Lula traded tired smiles and kept walking. Redantre's wounds had become infected, so Zane took his place bearing unconscious Czar. Sertina recovered and found she could limp along, leaning on Marko for support. The going was tiresome, as Czar slowed them down.

■■■

Tiki splashed across a mountain stream after taking a long drink of the refreshing and rejuvenating water. She scrambled up the bank and stopped to catch her breath. She had been trotting since sunrise. The sun now stood in the center of the sky. No clouds blocked the blinding light. Snow had fallen in the night and dusted the mountain tops. Tiki took a final deep breath and bounced back into a trot.

"I-," she panted. "I won't stop again until sunset. I can't lose ground."

With that, Tiki stretched her sore legs to canter. Her need pressed upon her weary heart. She tried to maintain speed as she bounded up a steep cliff. A loose rock slipped past her and knocked against her hoof.

Tiki grimaced and strained to keep her balance. Falling was *not* a possibility. She had too much at stake to stop. Finally pulling herself upright, Tiki trotted forward, glad to have that cliff out of her way. Another one loomed above her, but the challenge didn't daunt her for a minute. While she trotted, Tiki's eyes searched the rock face for any signs of an easier path. Not finding any, she began the grueling ascent up the peak.

■■

"Just a little further!" encouraged Comanche.

"Whew! I didn't know climbing mountains would be so much fun!" joked Stargazer cheerily.

"Well, now you know! And I'm most likely right to assume that you won't be wanting to do it very soon after we arrive in the grasslands?" chuckled Comanche.

"Never again!"

Everyone laughed. Czar thrashed about on Zane's back. The white colt trembled and tried to stay on his small hooves. The laughter stopped and silence thickened. Stargazer cautiously approached the sick stallion.

"Czar? Czar, wake up. It's me, Stargazer. Wake up!"

"I have to find her!" he gasped, still in a wild dream.

Sweat poured down his neck as he tossed and turned. The sharp movements gave Zane trouble standing. He braced his legs and lowered his head. Czar eventually stopped moving enough to allow Zane to stay balanced.

■ ■

Tiki fought back the urge to let her eyelids shut and forced herself to move. A rock stood in her way and she sighed. Her limbs were numb with pain and her stomach felt weak. She took another few steps and dropped her head. The rock was tall and she would have to jump it. Backing up three strides, Tiki burst into a canter. She pushed off the ground with her hind legs, seeming to pause in mid-air for a second before landing on the other side. Thundering away from the rock, Tiki ran until her legs gave out. She lay, panting, under a dying bush for protection. The bush covered her black and white coat completely. Anyone passing from outside would never notice her there. Thankful to be safe for the night, Tiki slept.

■ ■

Czar opened his eyes and looked about, delirious.

"Where am I? Tiki? Tiki! Where's Tiki? Is she safe?" he panicked, heart rate speeding up.

Stargazer heard him and quickly shot to his side. It was dark and Comanche had halted for the night. Not being able to sleep from worrying about Tiki, Stargazer was attentive to every noise.

"Czar! You're awake!" she exclaimed.

"Stargazer? Tiki!"

"Tiki isn't here," said Stargazer, unsure of how he would react.

"Of course. She went to find baskets at the human settlement before we leave for the mountain trek. Stargazer, would you try to find her for me? My legs feel too weak to travel just yet and I'm not sure why."

"Czar. We're in the mountains. We have no food, so Tiki went to find some. And to find the grasslands. You're very sick. Lie still and try to sleep," commanded Stargazer.

Czar obediently closed his eyes. He slipped into a dream.

Two pairs of eyes looked at him through the darkness. Glittering and cruel, they followed his every move. A noise accompanied them, like a soft patting against a hard surface. Growls came from the direction of the eyes.

"I'll attack from behind," snarled a voice.

"Good, good. It'll have no escape," snickered another.

"Watch yourself!" warned the first.

"I will. Horse meat is too rare in these parts to be missed. It'll be delicacies for us tonight!"

Tiki woke suddenly. The growls and snarls came closer. She shook with fear.

"Wolves!" she whispered to herself, wishing she had Czar with her.

Shaking the thought out of her mind, Tiki slowly stood, doing her best to stay undetected in the shadows. The first wolf lunged at her all at once. She jumped to the side, the beast falling on his face. A second charged at her and she fled. The blind flight through the dark was risky. Tiki could barely see two feet in front of herself, yet she didn't slow for a minute. The pursuer behind her grew quieter as he lost ground. His four padded paws had nothing on Tiki's four hard hooves as she galloped.

"Where do I go? What should I do?"

Tiki looked right and left, searching for some means of escape. No sound of pursuit reached her sensitive ears. Still determined to put some miles between her and the beasts, Tiki trotted silently to the left. After climbing over a small peak, she found a crevice made by two boulders wedged together. Her skinny body slid right into the crack and she had just enough room to stretch out her legs.

"Just for a few minutes. Then I'd best be up and out of here again," whispered Tiki to herself, shutting her eyes and resting her frightened mind.

~Chapter 9~
"Murderer"

Stargazer sighed. She still was unable to rest. Pacing back and forth, she surveyed the herd's state of health. Comanche's family was relatively strong, despite the food absence. Sertina and Arana were suffering more from loss of hope than of food. Lara and Marta kept to themselves, but not having their father with them for the painful journey starved them more than they could hide from everyone. Czar was the most ragged and careworn. Comanche opened his eyes and, seeing Stargazer pace out of the corner of his eye, got to his feet.

"It's early, Stargazer."

"I know. I can't sleep. What if she's hurt, Comanche?"

"Tiki?"

"Yes. We never should have let her go out alone. What were we thinking?"

"She's going to come back. She promised you,

didn't she? Tiki never breaks a promise once it's made. You need to stop worrying so much, Stargazer. It's not good for you. I wish you and the other foals could've had more time to play in the meadow, instead of getting dragged across an unknown mountain range to look for an unknown grassland."

"That's all right. Czar used to say everything 'happened for a reason'."

"Yes, he did. I wish he would wake and share more of his wisdom. He's a very thoughtful horse for his age. Only four, you know." Comanche shook his mane and laughed, trying to make Stargazer feel better. "I am *much* past that age and about a quarter as smart."

Stargazer tried to smile at him but couldn't. A strange feeling grew inside of her chest. She couldn't identify it. The sun finally crept back into place, though it was invisible to the herd. Clouds heavily laden with snow sank their spirits.

• •

Tiki slipped out of her hiding place and looked around. Eight inches of thick, heavy snow covered the ground.

"Well, this will make walking extra difficult," she sighed, shaking her head.

Picking her way through the shallower drifts, Tiki wandered hungrily out of the rockiest part of the small peak. At last, she reached the bottom. Before her stood yet another hill. But this one was very slight in incline. She plodded up it, thankful that it had a gentle slope. Her legs were numb from the freezing cold snow and her eyes stung from the dry air. Tiki reached the top of the hill and looked down. More small slopes were perceivable, though their heights were hard to judge because of the blowing snow. Something caught Tiki's eye, behind the hills.

"Is that- No, it can't be. Could that be the grasslands?" gaped Tiki.

Squinting her eyes and craning her neck to see, Tiki could barely make out a bright flash of green. The grasslands lay a few miles beyond the edge of the mountains. Exhaling in relief, Tiki cantered forward down the hill with an extra spring in her step. The work of running in the snow seemed to shrink as she inched closer and closer to her goal.

••

Stargazer hung her head. They had reached a huge drop-off and Comanche was desperately trying to find a way down the cliff. Her eyes watching the dirt, Stargazer spied a single set of tracks on the ground, leading between two large boulders.

"There! The snow must've fallen lightly here. I can see hoofprints! " she cried.

"What? Those could be Tiki's! We have to follow the tracks!" exclaimed Keiki.

Excitedly, the horses started to file through the space. Czar wheezed horribly and a drop of blood fell from his mouth. His eyes were squeezed shut, as if trying to stand the pain. Comanche laid back his ears and stopped the herd.

"We can't go on."

"Why not, Comanche? We know where to go. We also know that Tiki was here," pleaded Stargazer, not realizing Czar's condition.

"Look at Czar. Even if he was well, those prints

could be Mercury's. He could've traveled this way, behind Tiki. She probably passed here days ago!" explained Comanche.

"Mercury! Why, if he is following her, then he could be trying to get back at her! That horrible, scheming scoundrel!" fumed Stargazer, stamping her hoof angrily. "I hate him! He's always been an annoying little menace."

"Stargazer! Mind your tongue," snapped Sertina, seeing the horrified looks on Marta and Lara's faces.

"I'm sorry, but it's the truth! Comanche, what are we going to do about Czar? We *have* to go on! Mercury might be after Tiki at this moment!"

"Pull out the basket of herbs. I'll use what's left."

"Were you looking for this basket, *Comanche*?"

Stargazer closed her eyes at the sound of the sneering voice. Mercury, stepping out from behind the two boulders, threw his head back and let out a roar of arrogant laughter that chilled the filly's bones. He kicked the basket over the cliff and watched its contents flutter out onto the wind.

"Czar has *always* been the one to get in the way of me. I should have been chosen as leader! You'd all be better off without him. Tretaregon favored me over Czar, and you all know it. And how could he help it? I'm his nephew. Czar is no relation of his. He was an...*outcast* from an old herd that has long been dispersed. Czar, Redantre, Tretaregon and I are all that is left of those old bloodlines, though Czar is unworthy to be called one of us."

"And what did Czar ever do to be cast out by his own family?" asked Stargazer, who by this time was furious with Mercury.

"Well, didn't Tiki ever tell you? Oh, she did not, I see. I suppose she didn't want you to go around treating Czar like less than she thought he was, in spite of him be-,"

"Will you get to the point, Mercury?" shouted little Stargazer.

"There's no need to squeal, darling! Czar murdered his brother, in order to be next in line for leading the herd. Simple as that."

"That's a dirty lie! Czar would never do that, never!"

"He did, though. You know, Redantre's father might still be here if it wasn't for Czar."

"My mother said he died in an accident on the cliff!" cried Redantre, eyes filling and running over with tears.

"Is that what Czar told her? Oh, deary me! I didn't think he was as bad as all that, to tell his sister-in-law a lie!"

"Don't listen to him, foals. Czar said a tree fell across their path, breaking the bridge made by humans. His brother was behind him when it happened and slipped down," reassured Lula, hardly believing it to be true, but wanting the foals to be loyal to their leader.

"I was below the cliff when his brother fell! Czar kicked him over the cliff's edge. There was a shallow lake where we would swim and drink, right in the canyon. I was just finishing my afternoon swim when I heard a splash and saw the dead body in the lake. Czar realized I had seen it, and ran home. Of course, I headed him off and confronted him. Czar's father ordered him to leave. Tretaregon came of age soon after and started his own herd. He had pity on Czar and let him be a member, though he always told me that I was to be his heir."

Everyone suddenly understood Mercury and listened. His story was believable, compared to Czar never bringing it up. Stargazer hissed at Mercury.

"Go away, Mercury. You treacherous, deceitful, little liar!"

Stargazer was shaking with anger and Zane stepped in front of her to keep her from attacking the stallion. Mercury laughed at the sight.

"A filly, a *filly* will defend the dying stallion from the accusation of murder! And the rest of you stand silent before your leader!" he chortled.

"He's not dying!" screamed Stargazer, enraged. Tears spilled down her dirty nose. "How dare you come back to say that, Mercury!"

"You do not see how he suffers? Are you all blind? He is already gone! There is nothing you can do to save him!"

"I think he's right, Stargazer. We need to let him go. He is, after all, a murderer," Comanche whispered weakly.

Stargazer locked eyes with the gray stallion. A mixture of defeat, sadness, betrayal, and pain filled her eyes. She knew that Mercury would try to fight them if they didn't give in, but the herd was so weak.

"Listen to yourself, Comanche! Don't let Mercury speak lies into your head! You would really let Czar go? Let him die without a fight? Do you actually believe that Czar would kill his brother?" sobbed Stargazer.

Comanche lowered his neck and closed his eyes tightly.

"Mercury has always had a clear past. Czar liked to keep his past in the shadows. Now you know why. He's not going to make it, Stargazer. Accept it and move on."

"Stop it! Would you ju-."

"Comanche's right. We need to let him go, now that we know his crime. Tretaregon never, ever should have let him stay." Marko shook his head.

"We'll die if we don't get out of the mountains. Czar is just slowing us down. C'mon, Stargazer," said Sertina.

"I suppose I can forget all past times when you've wronged me and let you all be part of my new herd," sighed Mercury.

"Please, Mercury?" pleaded Arana. "We'll be ever so good to you!"

"But of course, darling filly! All who believe the truth about Czar are welcome."

Redantre knelt down in the snow and slid Czar off his back. He looked at Stargazer.

"Aren't you coming?"

"Redantre. Even you're deserting him," huffed Stargazer with a look of disgust.

"Stargazer, he killed my father! It's for your

own good, too. You'll die from one more day in this weather!"

"Is that what you're all worried about? Yourselves? I thought you were better than this. Don't you owe your lives to Czar?" cried Stargazer.

"No," jeered Mercury. "*Czar* owes his life to Redantre's family. Come on. If you want to die, stay with Czar. If you want a life of peace and freedom, without worry of a lying murderer for a leader, follow me."

Comanche, Lula, Marko, Arana, Sertina, Lara and Mercury started down the cliff. Redantre, Keiki, Zane, and Marta stood uncertainly around Stargazer and Czar.

"Keiki and Zane!" shouted Comanche. "Hurry up!"

"Marta! What are you doing?" asked Lara, trotting alongside her father.

"Redantre, don't leave me alone," whispered Stargazer. "Don't leave me."

"I won't. I promise."

"I'm staying," announced Keiki.

"So am I," said Zane.

"And me!" declared Marta.

Marko wheeled around and dashed back up to join the party.

"Count me in!"

"Thanks," smiled Stargazer. "Now, time for a plan."

● ●

Tiki gulped in the chilling air. The world around her was white and covered with new snow.

"Oh, no! I can't see the grasslands any longer!" she worried, whipping her head side to side to see.

She looked up and saw the stars peeking through the dark sky. One star, brighter and bigger than the rest, stood before her, blinking. It almost beckoned to her.

"The North Star."

Keeping her eyes up, Tiki plodded along in the

snow, following the North Star. Finally, when she could no longer stand, she found a ditch to lie in. The cold mud was frozen solid and not very comfortable to sleep on for the night. Tiki yawned and tucked her muzzle under her leg.

~Chapter 10~
"Ghost"

Czar opened his eyes for a split second, only to see a tiny, blurry figure pacing around the cliff. Stargazer shook with fear at the howls piercing the quiet.

"Zane, how close do you think the wolves are?"

"I don't know. Far enough to be safe, but too close for comfort. Don't worry. Try to get some sleep. I'll keep watch," he assured her.

"All right. Thank you."

"Goodnight!" called Keiki.

"I thought you were asleep!" jumped Marta, giggling.

"Nope!"

Keiki snuggled her withers into Marta's and the two fell asleep. Stargazer lay next to Czar and put her head on his shoulder.

"I wish Tiki was here. Then everything would

be right."

"She'll come back, Stargazer. Don't worry," yawned Marko.

Tiki wearily trudged up the slope of a hill. The light of the sun was blocked out by black clouds, creating a miserable landscape. A heavy wind blew snow in her eyes and pushed her off balance many times.

"Ugh!" huffed Tiki, climbing out of a snowdrift.

She snorted and continued her trek. The wind grew fiercer, as did the snow. Rain fell with the snow, freezing on the ground. Tiki slipped on the ice and skidded a few feet down the hill. Exhausted, she lay in the cold sleet until her strength returned. Using her hoof, Tiki uncovered a patch of wet grass and nibbled it slowly, savoring its salty taste. When she had finished eating, she shook her mane free of snow and trotted up the incline.

The top of the hill was flat and provided a clear view of the land. A frozen lake stretched across the white hills, making a boundary between the mountain country and the grasslands. The grasslands were still green and thriving, unlike the rest of the wintery world. Trees dotted the flat ground and flowers twisted up the tree trunks. Deer were grazing beside their young, birds sang cheerfully, and a pair of wild sheep ambled lazily about. The sun, still only barely showing, had started to set. Its vibrancy warmed Tiki's heart and soul.

"Beautiful, isn't it?"

Tiki jumped at the voice. Behind her, eight gray wolves had gathered in a semicircle. Their leader, a large white beast, sat right in the middle of the group.

"Who are you?" gulped Tiki.

"I am Ghost: Emperor of Fright, King of Wolves, and Terror of the Mountains. Would you like to hear the rest of my illustrious and flattering titles?"

Ghost tilted his shaggy head and looked Tiki in the eyes.

"N-no, thank you," she stammered fearfully.

"Please, let me introduce my companions. Grimlock, Rippingclaw, Poisonbite, Vipersting, Redeyes, Shadowpain, Gravedigger, and....Death!" he hissed, a cruel grin on his face.

Grimlock growled and Gravedigger pawed the ground. Ghost narrowed his black eyes at Tiki and she took a tiny step back.

"Come on, lads. Let's give this mare a souvenir she'll never forget!" he snickered. "You see, we don't like strangers in our land. When newcomers arrive, which is very rare because our glorious reputation, we deal very harshly with them. That is why you will never be able to warn your starving friends of the existence of the grasslands."

"What have you done to my friends?"

"Nothing yet. Besides, killing you will be enough to kill them, won't it?"

Tiki's throat tightened and tears threatened to spill from her eyes. Ghost cackled.

"Shadowpain? Are you ready?"

"Always, Master. Always."

Before he had even the slightest chance to attack, Tiki bolted. Galloping hard, she breezed down the hill, past the frozen lake, and into the grasslands. Her flight scared flocks of wild birds off a pond and startled a fawn and her mother.

"You can run, but you'll never escape!" yelled Ghost, close behind her.

Tiki's hooves pounded the soft, grassy ground as she fled. She could feel the air become warmer and warmer. Her breaths came and went with effort and bits of foam from her mouth splattered on her chest. Suddenly, she tripped. One of her hooves had caught in a rabbit hole as she ran. Ghost laughed.

"Did you really think you had a chance, mare?"

The eight other wolves chimed in with their various sneering remarks. Tiki got whiplash from turning her head so fast to find the owner of each hideous voice. Redeyes bristled the fur on his neck and his red eyes gleamed in the waning light. Vipersting snarled, showing off rows and rows of fierce and sharp-looking teeth. Grimlock, an enormous wolf that almost rivaled the monstrosity of Ghost, crouched on the ground, writhing from left to right. Tiki shuddered as drool dropped from Poisonbite's mouth and pooled on the dirt.

"As I was saying earlier before our little game of tag, Shadowpain will give us an entertaining show."

Shadowpain disappeared into the shadows of the trees and Tiki peered around her to find the nasty beast. A gray blur flew at her and knocked her over. Tiki's back and legs hurt dreadfully but she did not show Ghost how much pain she was in. Shadowpain returned to Ghost's side.

"Oh, I see how it is for you. You're used to pain. But we're just warming up. Poisonbite!"

"Yes?"

"Do your....*magic*!"

"Of course, milord."

Poisonbite paced around Tiki. Her eyes never left the disgusting jaws that he continually snapped open and shut. The wolf jumped at her and bit her shoulder. Tiki screamed in agony as the sharp teeth tore the skin and skimmed the muscle beneath. Ghost just laughed.

"Well done, Poisonbite, well done. We have trained you very well indeed. Vipersting," said Ghost.

Vipersting, a terrifying animal with light green eyes, sidled up to Tiki. He spat on her already painful wound.

"Stop!" sobbed Tiki.

The spit from Vipersting's mouth stung and smarted. Tiki thrashed on the ground to relieve the pain. Rippingclaw stepped over her, his longs claws shining in the moonlight.

"When I'm done with you, you'll wish I had just killed you," he whispered into her ear.

Tiki tried to understand what he meant, but a terrible feeling shattered through her body. The wolf's claws sliced her back open and dug deep. He scraped the skin away, revealing tightened muscles and bone. Tiki shrieked. The pain was unbearable. Redeyes locked eyes with her. A burning sensation followed, almost as if the flaming red beams were searing their way into her heart. She tried with all the strength she could muster to look away, but he hypnotized her mind with his eyes.

"That's enough, Redeyes!" announced Ghost. "We want her to feel *everything*, remember? Too bad she won't be able to warn her petty little friend about us. Grimlock. Entertain us."

"I'm ready," he growled.

Moaning and shaking, Tiki turned her head to see her next attacker. He pounced on her and gripped her neck in his mouth. Although he had no teeth, the air was forced out of Tiki's lungs. She kicked at him but the lack of air soon began to weaken her greatly.

"Stargazer! I need to-I-I-say good-bye!" she choked out, starting to lose consciousness.

Grimlock dropped her head from his mouth. She gasped and the air filled her lungs once again. Gravedigger approached and picked her frail body up in his mouth. The strange party walked for a few yards to a pile of rocks. Ghost and the rest drew back. Gravedigger threw Tiki as far as he could out onto the rocky ground.

"Czar! Where are you? Please, help me! Make them stop!" she screamed, tumbling down the rock pile.

Her once black and white coat was completely red with her blood. She couldn't move. Ghost marched over to her.

"Gravedigger seems to have found the perfect place for you to live out your final moments and to lie quiet in the waiting years before the earth cracks and is consumed in fire. Are you comfortable? Death is very ready to finish this, if you are. If not, I think I could help you want to see him."

"I don't want to die," whimpered Tiki, trembling in fear.

"Oh, I understand," said Ghost with mock-sympathy.

"No, you don't!"

Tiki lifted her head and caught his eye. The pain made her nauseous.

"You don't understand because you only live for the blood of innocent lives! Y-you don't care about anything other than terrorizing the animals around you. I have to return to my herd! I have a new future waiting for me and my friends. I promised Stargazer I'd come back. I never break my promises."

"She's quite oblivious to the fact that a grave is the only future she has." Ghost shook his head.

"Just let me go!"

"And you think I'm going to listen to you?" retorted Ghost.

A flash across the sky warned the group of an oncoming storm. Rain fell in sheets, soaking the wolves and Tiki. Ghost howled in frustration.

"Let's go, lads. We'll finish her tomorrow, if she's still alive."

~Chapter 11~
"Nightmare"

Stargazer shivered in the dark. The rain had drenched the herd of colts and fillies, which hadn't moved since Mercury took away the other horses. Redantre was getting weak with fatigue and Keiki had a nasty cough. Marko complained every five minutes of his hunger. Stargazer had just settled down when a heart-wrenching scream echoed into her ears, carried by the wind.

"Tiki!"

The voice was immediately recognizable, though the tone rose in horror and pain. Stargazer nosed Czar.

"Czar! Wake up! Please!" she begged.

He didn't answer and Stargazer slumped down with the rain beating against her back.

∎∎

Tiki drew a raspy breath.

"It's pointless to try. I'm dead already. Ghost will be here soon, along with...Death," she shuddered. "Give it up, Tiki. You'll never make it."

Closing her eyes, Tiki tried to imagine what life in the grasslands would've been like, already accepting death as the victor. Instead, she saw Czar.

He lay on his side, taking short and shallow breaths. A deep pit lay a foot away from him. The pit was full of darkness; horrifying and bone-chilling shrieking and crying came from within. Slowly but very steadily, Czar slipped inch by inch to the edge of the pit of death. He struggled as much as he could in his condition to stop, but could not.

"No! He can't die!"

Tiki shook herself out of the nightmare and tried to get up. Her legs buckled and she fell. Again and again she lifted herself up, only to fall. The rocks beneath her scratched the delicate skin on her legs, but Tiki didn't care. After two more attempts, she finally stood. Still fearing the return of Ghost and his minions, Tiki hurried along at a walk. It took thirty minutes to cover one yard and she started to lose her balance.

Czar cried out for Tiki as a black human hand

reached out of the pit, grasping for him.

Tiki steadied herself and broke into a trot. The grass was still wet from the rain and she slipped, falling down. Blood stained the ground where she fell.

"Pull yourself together, Tiki. Czar needs you, even if you die in the end."

A large eagle's nest was on the grass beside her.

"It must've fallen off the tree," she figured.

She filled it with mouthfuls of grass and flowers to bring back. The pain she experienced from just bending down to pluck the flowers from their stems was excruciating. Tiki seized the nest up in her mouth. The scratchy straw irritated her muzzle and made her want to drop it. She grimly remembered that Ghost would be returning and pushed her body forward.

A numb feeling overtook her as she walked. She saw flashes of memories from the meadows. Stargazer's voice rose above the rest, her sweet gentleness comforting to Tiki:

"Czar found them. He told me you were upset and asked if there was anything you would want. I said you loved dandelions, and he left Mercury in charge so he could search for some. He must have been really desperate to have him be in charge. Here, take them."

Czar galloped through her mind. He chased valiantly after Kentril and Tretaregon while they were being led away by settlers.

"Tiki, they are taking your father! Don't you care? Don't you care that these outsiders, these two-legged menaces, are taking away your father, as well as Tretaregon? What will happen to the herd if Tretaregon and Kentril are gone? We will be leaderless! Step aside!"

Tiki shook her mind clear of the vivid memories.

"No good stopping to relive old memories when my friends need help," she said.

More rain fell on Tiki. Tears of misery mixed with the downpour from the sky, to utterly soak the mare. She trudged up the hill where she had first met Ghost and his friends. Seeing the rest of the troubling terrain standing before her, Tiki became discouraged.

"Where is she?!" roared a loud, growling voice in the lands behind.

"Ghost!" whispered Tiki fearfully.

She forced her numb legs to canter down the hill. Gaining momentum, she steadily raced up the next incline. The pain strangely subsided as she ran, and she prayed it would continue to be so.

••

Stargazer closed her eyes in sadness, letting a tear slide loose. She lay at Czar's side. He was barely breathing and Stargazer knew he was almost gone. Her voice cracked as she spoke.

"Tiki, if you're out there...please hurry. We need you."

She dropped her head and cried silently, skinny form shaking with noiseless sobs. The wind whirled around her and whisked her away to the happy days of playing in the meadow.

••

Tiki fought to keep upright. A fierce wind was blowing from the north and her legs were not strong enough to withstand the force of it. Trotting up a steep path, she recognized places that she had passed on her way to the grasslands. The nest in her mouth was beginning to feel very heavy and slowed her progress.

"Just a little farther before I have a rest," she sighed, lifting her hooves and placing them with care.

No sooner had the words left her mouth, something horrible flashed in her mind.

The black hand settled tightly around Czar's barrel and started dragging him to the brink of the pit.

Tiki trembled and kept going. The wind increased and many times, pushed Tiki off her hooves and onto sharp rocks. Her skin become covered in even more scratches and her body was weak.

"Czar, just hold on. I'm coming!" she shouted above the wind.

His face branded in her mind, Tiki trotted on. She found little paths winding through the peaks.

They protected her from the wind for a few minutes at a time and saved her the long hike up the steep hills.

• •

Stargazer woke up to a sickening feeling in her stomach. Turning on her side, she looked over at Czar. His body was still. Stargazer choked when she saw his open, glazed eyes.

"Czar, you can't leave. Not now. Not when I need you the most. What will I do without you? Tiki isn't here, the rest of the horses are sick, and you're..."

She shook her head, trying to clear her mind of confusion.

~Chapter 12~
"Almost"

Tiki slipped as she tried to walk up a steep pile of rock.

"Ahhh!" she cried.

Blood ran down her legs and she looked to see that the wounds that Rippingclaw had created were opened. Lying down, Tiki rested her head on her knees.

Czar's front legs began to disappear into the black pit, the hand still encircling his body. His screams for Tiki slowly echoed away, diminishing to a faint moaning and crying.

Tiki lifted her head and let a neigh loose, not caring if Ghost was still tracking her and might hear. The pain from the noise burned her throat and gave excruciating pain throughout her body.

"Czar! Stargazer! I'm almost there! Hang on just a little bit longer!"

■■

Stargazer jumped to her feet in surprise when she heard the voice rising above the wind.

"Tiki's almost here! She's coming to save Czar!" she exclaimed, ecstatic.

"Really? Do you think it's really her?" gasped Keiki, coughing.

"It's gotta be her." Redantre grew excited.

"Finally! I'm sooo hungry!" moaned Marko.

Marta twitched in her sleep, hearing their conversation, but was too weak to lift her own voice.

∙∙

Trotting with her muzzle about to brush the ground, Tiki wearily trudged up another rise in terrain. Her chest squeezed tightly and she began to think she would die before she got back to Czar. She coughed hoarsely.

"I can't feel my legs anymore!" panicked Tiki. "The snow is so cold, it's numbing my body.

Tiki coughed again, this time falling to her knees from the pain it brought. The nest fell out of her mouth, almost spilling. She heaved it back up and shivered forward. Nothing around her seemed familiar.

"No! I must've gone the wrong way!"

Turning ninety degrees, Tiki snorted tiredly and walked in the other direction. Coughing and stumbling, she traveled until a high wall stopped her.

"*That* wasn't here a few days ago. And since mountains don't sprout walls and grow rock and stone, I'm going to assume that I should've kept going on the first path."

Tiki shifted her direction to back the way she had come and trotted to make up the wasted time, though her legs barely felt the quick movements. It soon became hard to swallow, and Tiki found she was gasping for breath.

"What's wrong with you, Tiki? You're fine! Now get along!" she heard herself scold.

Sidestepping a rock, she tripped up a tiny peak. Whenever she tried to stop, Czar slipped another inch into the pit of death. Already exhausted beyond imagination, Tiki fell and rolled down the other side of the hill. No strength returned to her as she lay in the deep snow. Before she had to witness Czar teeter on the brink of death, Tiki forced herself to standing.

"I *must* go on."

She recognized a few places she had passed on her way to the grasslands. Taking heart, Tiki turned her face to the wind and took a step.

■■

Stargazer watched, terrified, as Czar began to choke and stop breathing momentarily.

"No. No, Czar, no! Don't leave me! Please!" she whispered.

Marko's stomach growled loudly. Keiki wheezed. Redantre was trying hard to sleep, but Marta and Zane were grumbling next to him and made it almost impossible to block out the noise. None of them realized what was going on. Stargazer watched each of her tears roll off her muzzle and splash on the rocks. They came faster and bigger as Czar's breaths came slower and shorter. She sniffed and let out a long sigh of sadness.

"I just wish it didn't have to end this way."

■■

Tiki dug her back hooves into the ground,

sliding to a stop. A very hard climb lay before her.
Two boulders sat a few feet apart from each
other, and Tiki remembered how an eagle had
shown her the way down. But now, looking at the
hill for what it really was, she felt discouraged.
The path was almost vertical. In the state of
health that Tiki was in, it would be hard to
conquer. Taking a long, deep breath, Tiki walked
forward, her movements robotic. Pain rippled
through her body as she moved. The cuts and
bites on her care-worn body were healing, but still
infected and painful. She groaned and tried to
move again. Her heart beat quickly and sweat
poured down her back as she tripped forward. A
few feet up the path, Tiki lost her footing and fell
to the bottom again. More deep wounds scarred
the stained and dirty coat. She started to feel
dizzy and sick with fatigue. Planting her hooves
apart, Tiki rested her muzzle on the ground. Her
mind slowly cleared and stopped swirling about.
Another squeezing pain in her chest told Tiki that
she would likely not be able to travel the path.

*The front half of Czar's body disappeared
completely into the darkness.*

"Stop!" Tiki screamed aloud to her mind.

The yell took up most of her barely remaining strength. She pushed her weak frame to move and winced at the pain it gave her. Blissful sleep was awaiting, she continually reminded herself. Soon. Not yet, but soon.

••

Stargazer tried to sleep, her stomach twisting hungrily. Keeping her eyes turned to the path between the two boulders, she watched and waited and hoped. Marta yawned and gave Stargazer a sad smile.

"Have you heard her again?"

"No, Marta. Nothing. I'm worried."

"Try to get some rest, Stargazer. You've been restless and haven't been sleeping. You will want all your strength for when Tiki gets back and we continue on," reminded Marta, voice gentle and tired.

"All right. Good night," sighed Stargazer.

"Good night."

••

Tiki's nose itched from the straw nest in her

mouth. Most of the grasses and flowers from the grasslands were still lying in the bottom. The climb was wearing on her and she kept dropping the nest.

"At least there's something of worth in it," she grumbled.

The boulders drew steadily nearer with every few minutes. Squinting her eyes, Tiki peered curiously at a tiny shadow sitting just beyond the exit of the path.

"Stargazer? Is that you?" whispered Tiki, barely making a noise.

"Tiki!"

Stargazer jumped up and stood in between the boulders. Tiki bounded forward, not even feeling the pain of her sensitive wounds. Stargazer buried her head in Tiki's tattered mane.

"Oh, it's you, it's you, it's really you!" wept Stargazer in excited astonishment.

"Yes, it's me. Where's Czar? Is he all right?"

"He's over here, Tiki."

Stargazer solemnly led Tiki over to where Czar lay. His breaths were not visible and Tiki feared that she was indeed too late.

"Czar? Czar, it's me; Tiki."

"Is he....de-dead?" trembled Stargazer.

"I don't know."

Tiki pulled grass from her basket and held it out in front of her. Czar's nostrils twitched as the spiky green grass tickled his lips. Startled, Tiki jerked back, bracing herself against the pain.

"Oh, no! Tiki, you're hurt!" gasped Stargazer.

"Yes, Stargazer. I'm not well. I need rest and food. But Czar is more important," she insisted.

Tiki nudged Czar and offered the grass again. Stargazer helped Tiki to mash up the grass and drench it in water, turning it into a pasty green liquid. They opened Czar's mouth and dropped the liquid inside. He swallowed. Tiki repeated the process all through the night. Finally, Czar's eyelids fluttered open.

"Tiki?"

"Czar!"

He managed a weary smile.

"I thought I had died," said Czar.

"So did I. I've been so worried about you!" sniffed Tiki, tears running down her dirty coat.

She leaned into him and cried quietly, just glad to be with him. Stargazer approached.

"Tiki, you need to rest. Let me clean your cuts."

Too weak to do anything but nod, Tiki allowed Stargazer to help her find a place to sleep. She closed her eyes, enjoying the peacefulness of the night. Suddenly, another sharp pain pressed against her heart. This one was worse than any of the pains she had felt during the wolf attack or the journey home. Gasping for breath, Tiki started to choke and cough. She knew she had only a couple seconds. Stargazer turned around, hearing the hoarse wheezing.

"Tiki!" screamed Stargazer.

"Star-g-azer, I l-l-ove you. The grasslands-through

boulders-straight. Ghost-b-beware!" coughed Tiki.

Her breath caught in her throat. All at once, Tiki's bright ocean-blue eyes turned dull and glassy. She dropped her head and exhaled. Stargazer waited for her to close her eyes. Tiki never did. She never even blinked. She fell asleep that night, lying on the cold stone, never to wake again.

~Chapter 13~
"Home"

Stargazer took a deep breath and looked up. What she saw delighted her sorrowful, downcast eyes. The grasslands were everything she had wished and dreamed of. No snow covered the flowering hills, fresh smells filled every nick and cranny in the land, and fruit grew on each tree.

"We're here," she exhaled.

"We are, Stargazer. We are."

Czar stood beside her, once again strong and healthy. Stargazer smiled happily, though an ache in her heart reminded her of Tiki. Poor Tiki. Already unwell when she made the journey to find food and the grasslands, the pretty black and white paint Mustang had not survived even a full day after arriving back with the remaining members of the herd. Stargazer cleared her mind of sad thoughts and caught Czar's eyes. A twinkle shone in them that she had missed for a very long time. She took off galloping with Czar shouting behind.

"Get back here!" he roared, trying to gain ground.

"Never!" giggled Stargazer.

She gave a deafening neigh and charged ahead. Dashing over tall grass and flowers, they galloped to a large lake.

"Let's go in!"

Stargazer nodded, too busy catching her breath to reply. Czar shot past her and splashed into the lake. Water flew everywhere and soaked his coat. Its dark liver chestnut coloring returned from beneath the mountain grime and he looked much more like himself. Stargazer leapt in, disappearing briefly under the foamy water. The mud slowly washed off, showing her gorgeous blue roan coat. She laughed and drank of the crystal clear water.

"Oh, it's so sweet and good!"

"Stargazer, I do believe this could be the land where dreams come true," remarked Czar thoughtfully.

Stargazer wondered for a minute at the

strange, sad shadow that fell over Czar's face. Then it vanished, almost as fast as it had appeared. She clambered out of the lake, flashing back to the day when Czar and Tiki had taken Comanche's foals and herself to the little stream in the woods. They had climbed to a small, solitary cliff and taken in its serene beauty. Upon their return, the group had witnessed the capture of Kentril, Tiki's father, and Tretaregon, the former herd leader. Czar's election as the new leader had almost been unanimous. Stargazer shook her mane free of water and her mind free of the old memories.

"Hey! Stop that!" laughed Czar.

The water from her mane had gotten all over him.

"You already were wet," she reminded him.

"There's Redantre! Come on!"

Czar cantered over to his friend. Stargazer gave a last flying buck before running to join them.

"Thank you, Tiki," she said aloud while

galloping. "for giving up your bright future here so the rest of us could run wild and free. I will never forget you, Tiki."

Stargazer whinnied and reared up on one of the hilltops, her form silhouetting against the setting sun. A familiar, loving voice whispered through the wind into her ear:

"I'm here, Stargazer. Be brave. Stand strong."

RUN WILD

ABOUT THE AUTHOR

~

N. D. Ableson, age 13, loves horses and horseback riding. Her writing inspirations include J.R.R. Tolkien and J.K. Rowling. Some of her non-writing hobbies are playing the cello, reading, and collecting model horses.

www.ingramcontent.com/pod-product-compliance
Lightning Source LLC
Chambersburg PA
CBHW020521290526
45786CB00002B/713